The Wild Imagination of Willy Nilly

THE FASTEST KID IN THE WORLD

WRITTEN & DESIGNED BY CHRIS STEAD

ILLUSTRATIONS BY RONZKIE

BOOK III

First Published in 2017 by Old Mate Media

Text and Images Copyright © 2020 Old Mate Media

No text or images may be reproduced wholly or in part in any form of media without prior written permission from the creator, Chris Stead, of Old Mate Media. The characters, setting and story are fictional and were created in full by Chris Stead, owner of Old Mate Media. The entire contents of this book are the copyright of Old Mate Media. The Wild Imagination of Willy Nilly and Willy Nilly Adventures are trademarks of Old Mate Media.

SECOND EDITION

ISBN = 978-1-925638-51-6

CONNECT WITH US

 FACEBOOK.COM/OLDMATEMEDIA   @OLDMATEMEDIA  WWW.OLDMATEMEDIA.COM   @OLDMATEMEDIA   BOOKS@OLDMATEMEDIA.COM

HOW TO USE THE WILLY NILLY BOOKS IN A LEARNING CONTEXT

RECOMMENDED FOR STAGE 1 (YEARS 1 AND 2)

Chris Stead's Fastest Kid in the World is reminiscent of Maurice Sendak's Where the Wild Things Are in that it intimately follows the adventures of a young boy with a wild imagination into an exciting fantasy world. Albeit one derived from normal activities.

Picture books like Fastest Kid in the World and Where the Wild Things Are allow students to consider how combining visual and printed texts to tell a story can achieve a deeper understanding of a text's allegorical and symbolic significance. On this page you will find some activities you can use with Fastest Kid in the World in the classroom or at home.

OUTCOMES TAKEN FROM THE ENGLISH K-10 SYLLABUS
| BY SCHOOL KINDERGARTEN TEACHER SARAH NELSON

FOR PARENTS AND TEACHERS: DRAWING CONNECTIONS BETWEEN SIMILAR TEXTS:

Stage 1 – English – Reading and Viewing 1: Discuss different texts on a similar topic, identifying similarities and differences between the stories. Read Fastest Kid in the World in conjunction with one of the classics below and ask your children to point out the similarities in theme and imagery between the two.

TITLE	AUTHOR	CONNECTING THEME
Where the Wild Things Are	Maurice Sendak	Imagination
McElligot's Pool	Dr. Seuss	Imagination
All the World	Liz Garton Scanlon	Beach, Family

FOR PARENTS: CRITICAL THINKING SKILLS

Research has shown that enjoying a book with your child each night has great benefits on their ongoing development of both their reading and comprehension skills. Below are a number of questions you can ask your child before reading, while reading and after reading to help them critically evaluate the images and words on the page. Stead's Fastest Kid in the World is particularly effective, because the image is not obscured by the text.

BEFORE READING
Look at the cover and ask what they think the story will be about.* Flip to the first page. Without revealing the text, ask your child what they think is happening on the page. Elaborate on what your child says; ask, "what is it about the picture that makes you think that?" Once they've given their evaluation, reveal the text and discuss how close their analysis was to the actual story. Point to a character's face (preferably showing joy or sadness) and ask your child to identify how the character is feeling.

WHILE READING
What is the main idea of the story? Ask, "what do you think this story is about?" Find words your child may not know on the page and ask what they think it could mean given the context of the story. Ask your child if they can explain the plot (problem, obstacle, resolution etc.) before revealing the text. Predict and discuss* what is happening in each scene.

AFTER READING
Explore the author's intent. Ask, "why do you think the author wrote this book? To entertain or inform?"** Ask your child to summarise the events from Fastest Kid in the World.***

* **Stage 1 – English – Thinking imaginatively and creatively:** Predict and discuss ideas drawn from picture and digital books.
** **Stage 1 – English – Reading and viewing 2:** Discuss possible author intent and intended audience of a range of texts.
*** **Stage 1 – English – Reading and viewing 1:** Sequence a summary of events and identify key facts or key arguments in imaginative, informative and persuasive texts.

DEDICATED TO

KATE + CHARLIE + JASMINE + PATRICK

Willy Nilly really loves fast cars.

Big, colourful ones that do long skids and huge jumps.

"C'mon," he would whisper to his dog whenever his dad wasn't looking.

Then he would sneak into the driver's seat of the family car and pretend to race.

VROOOOM!!

One day, Willy Nilly's dad barged into his room with a really cool idea.

"Hey Willy," his dad asked, "do you want to build a billycart?"

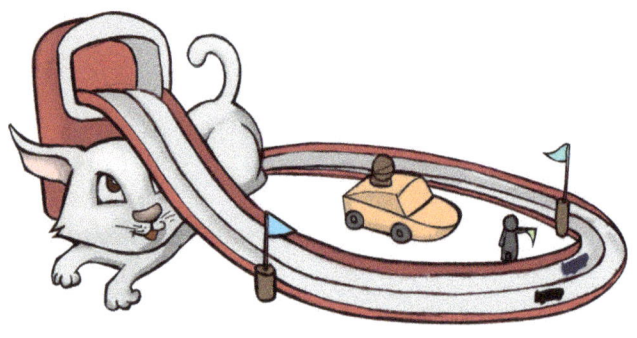

"Yeah, that would be awesome!" SHOUTED Willy, JUMPING up and down EXCITEDLY.

So, they raced out the door and got to work straight away.

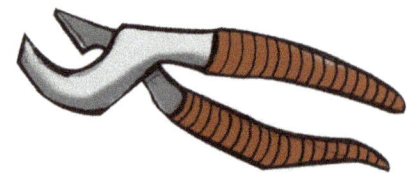

First, they found a large piece of wood to use as the bottom.

Then they used a hammer and some bolts to put on the tyres.

BANG! BANG! BANG!

Next they used a drill to screw on a seat and a steering wheel.

Finally, they painted it red and put a number 4 sticker on the side, just like a race car.

It was an AWESOME billykart! They simply had to take it to the park and try it out.

Willy's dad pushed him down the path, but he wasn't able to do any big skids.

"Sorry Willy," his dad said, "I'm trying, but I just can't push you fast enough."

"There's a real race happening in town tomorrow; we'll go and watch that instead."

But Willy couldn't wait. That night he was trying to fall asleep when he had a brilliant idea.

"What if I put soap on the wheels," he told his dog. "That would make them slippery."

"And what if I took the kart to the top of the biggest hill in town? Then I could go really fast?"

His dog loved the idea. So, he SNUCK slowly into the bathroom to find some soap.

The next day, Willy took the soap and his billycart up the biggest hill in town.

He then RUBBED soap onto each of its four tyres to make them super slippery.

Willy put on his helmet, took one big breath, and gave his dog a high five.

"Here I come!" he SHOUTED. "The fastest kid in the world!"

You will never guess what happened next!

Willy had put WAAAAYYYY too much soap on the wheels.

Suddenly he was flying down the hill so fast he could barely hold on.

His hair was BLOWING everywhere, and his eyes were beginning to water.

When he got to a big right-hand corner, Willy was going too fast to turn.

He went straight ahead towards some workers painting a big sign bright blue.

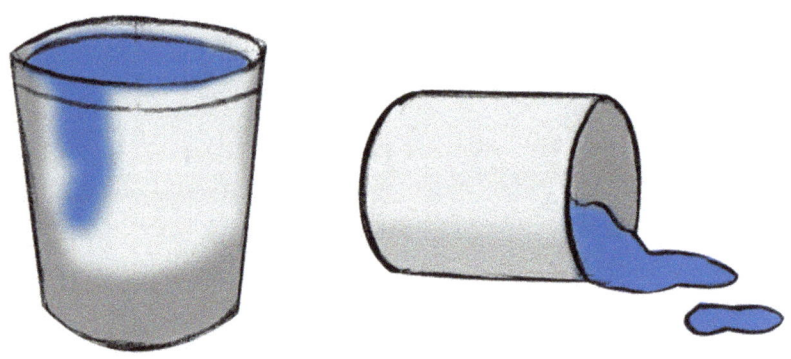

SMASH! He went crashing through the sign and it exploded into bits.

Then blue paint SPLASHED over everything, everywhere.

On the other side was a busy footpath and people diving out of the way.

He YANKED the wheel hard to the right and just missed a tall skinny person.

Then he PULLED it hard to the left and just dodged a fat short person.

Before going straight between two LEAPING dogs. "Watch out!" Willy yelled.

BOOM! Willy burst beyond a fence and into someone's backyard.

He went straight through a clothesline and got covered in all the washing.

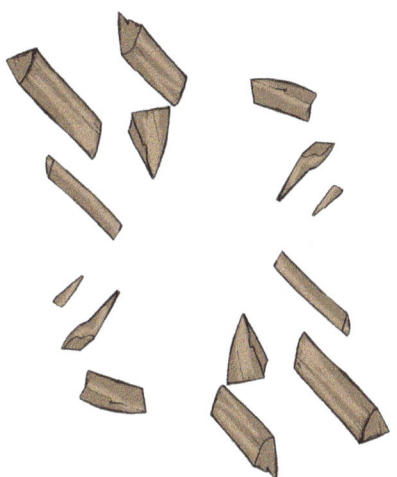

"Move out of the way!" he SCREAMED as a bed sheet wrapped across his eyes.

Before he ZIPPED through an open gate and out onto a busy street.

"Oh no," cried Willy! "There's cars and motorbikes and trucks and a fire engine."

He WEAVED between the traffic as fast as he could.

Willy kept pressing his horn extra hard. Beep! Beeeppp!

BEEEEEEPPPPP!

Until he spotted a turn-off that went into the park and towards the lake.

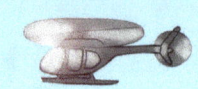

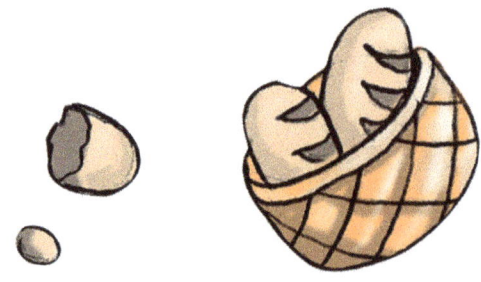

Willy was going superfast now. He was going faster than any boy had ever been before.

SPEEDING past the football fields, under the trees and all the way down to the lake.

He was going so fast near the water he created his own wave.

WHOOSSHH!

It SPLASHED over all the ducks and blew a hat right off a poor granny.

Then do you know what he saw? A DEAD END! The path ended in a big pile of dirt.

He couldn't turn in time as he was going way too fast.

"Argghhhh!"

Willy went right off the jump and HURTLING through the air.

Higher than the houses and the trees and even the birds.

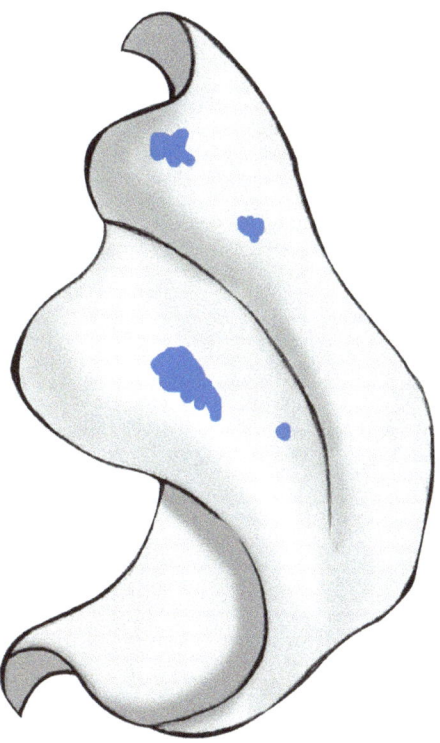

"What now?" wondered Willy as he looked desperately for a landing spot.

That's when he saw the racetrack with cars speeding for the finish line.

Willy landed right on the main straight at a BREAKNECK pace.

In fact, he passed everyone and went into first place.

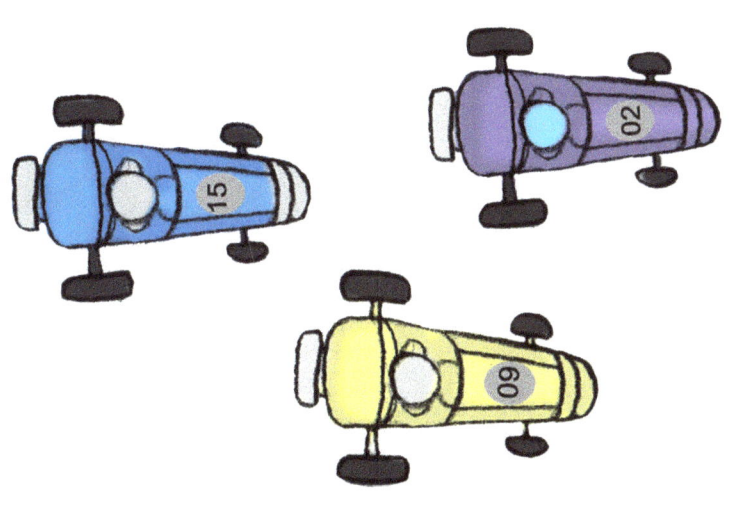

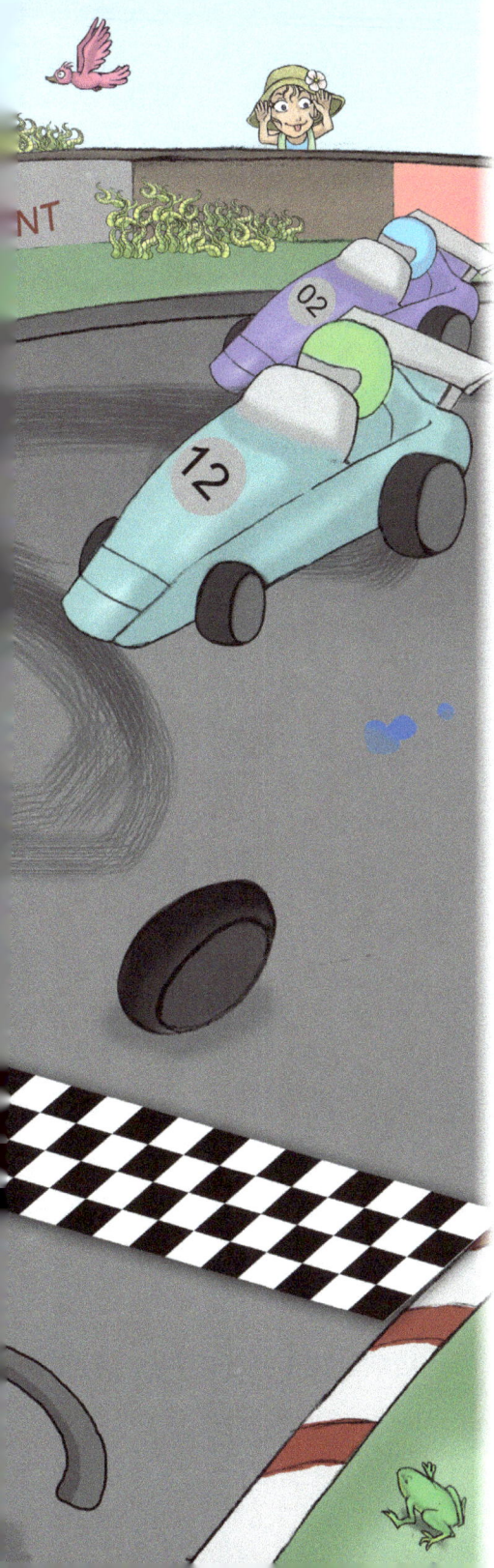

With one final big pull of the steering wheel Willy turned his billycart sharply to the left.

It spun once, twice, then three times before STOPPING in a cloud of smoke.

Plus, it left the biggest skid mark Willy had ever seen.

The crowd went crazy, CHEERING and CLAPPING as loud as it could.

So, that's how Willy Nilly became the fastest kid in the world.

It's also how he set a record for the BIGGEST billycart jump and skid of all time.

And it not only explains how Willy got first place in the Racing Championship.

But also, why the race ended with his dad yelling...

"Willy, you're in so much trouble!"

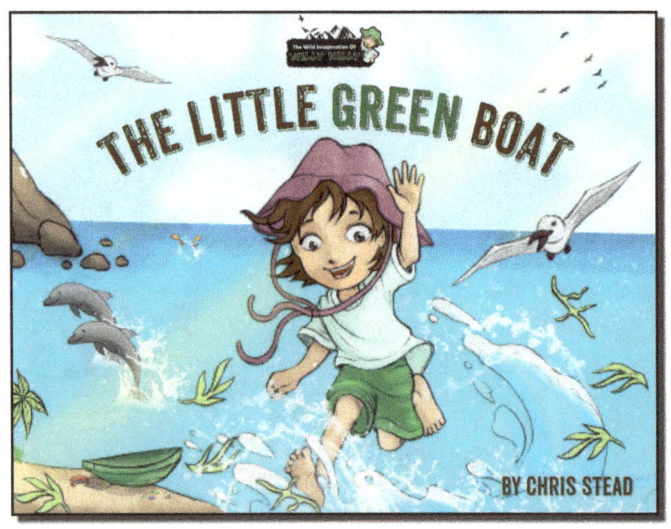

DISCOVER MORE BOOKS BY CHRIS STEAD

THE WILD IMAGINATION OF WILLY NILLY SERIES

AND MANY MORE TITLES – VISIT OLDMATEMEDIA.COM

www.ingramcontent.com/pod-product-compliance
Lightning Source LLC
Chambersburg PA
CBHW051254110526
44588CB00026B/2995